FACT FRENZY
SPACE

THE STARS

Lisa Regan

PowerKiDS press.

Published in 2021 by
The Rosen Publishing Group, Inc.
29 East 21st Street, New York, NY 10010

Cataloging-in-Publication Data

Names: Regan, Lisa.
Title: The stars / Lisa Regan.
Description: New York : PowerKids Press, 2021. | Series:
Fact frenzy: space | Includes glossary and index.
Identifiers: ISBN 9781725320321 (pbk.) | ISBN
9781725320345 (library bound) | ISBN 9781725320338
(6 pack)
Subjects: LCSH: Stars--Juvenile literature. | Galaxies--
Juvenile literature.
Classification: LCC QB801.7 R465 2021 | DDC 523.8--dc23

Copyright © Arcturus Holdings Ltd, 2021

Manufactured in the United States of America

CPSIA Compliance Information: Batch CSPK20: For Further Information contact
Rosen Publishing, New York, New York at 1-800-237-9932.

Find us on

Contents

THE HUBBLE TELESCOPE SEES STARS BEING BORN

The Hubble Space Telescope was launched in 1990 from the Discovery space shuttle. It travels around Earth taking incredible pictures of very, very far-off objects and events.

How far?

The Hubble Telescope can see objects 13 billion light-years away. A light-year is the distance that light travels in one year—that's 5.9 trillion miles (9.5 trillion km), which is like looping around Earth 237 million times. Now multiply that by 13 billion—it's almost impossible to imagine how far that distance really is!

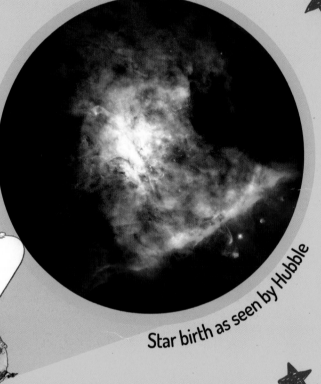

Star birth as seen by Hubble

Quick, look! I think a star is being born!

THE HUBBLE TELESCOPE IS POWERED ENTIRELY BY THE SUN.

The Hubble Space Telescope circling Earth.

Seeing clearly

Telescopes on Earth have to look through the clouds and gases of our planet's atmosphere to see out into space. This seriously limits how far they can see. In its position around 340 miles (547 km) above Earth, Hubble can see straight out into space without this hazy atmosphere getting in the way. This means it can see incredibly faint objects very far off into space.

Built for accuracy

In order to take pictures of such faint, distant objects, Hubble has to be incredibly accurate. It is built to keep very steady, which helps it find an object and take a picture of exactly where it is. The amount to which it ever wavers its view to either side of an object is about the same as the width of a human hair seen from one mile (1.6 km) away.

FACT 2

The telescope is named after Edwin Hubble, who discovered that there are other galaxies beyond our own Milky Way.

Edwin Hubble was a talented athlete and basketball coach, as well as a famous astronomer.

Perfect mirrors

The Hubble Telescope uses a system of perfectly lined-up mirrors to see deep into space. These mirrors are very precisely made to ensure that they can see things as accurately as possible. Hubble's main mirror is so finely polished that if you scaled it up to be as wide as Earth, there wouldn't be any bumps more than around 6 inches (15 cm) tall.

THERE ARE AROUND 70 BILLION TRILLION STARS

If you counted up every single grain of sand in all the deserts and beaches on Earth, it would still be less than the number of stars in the known universe.

Stars and galaxies

In our galaxy, the Milky Way, there are more than 300 billion stars—that's 40 times as many stars as there are people on Earth. Scientists believe there are around 100 billion galaxies in the known universe. Some are much smaller than ours, but the total number of stars in the universe is so big it's hard to really imagine it.

I thought we stars were special?

Sorry, pal, we're pretty common!

FACT 4

Using a basic telescope on a clear, dark night, you could see up to 2.65 million stars!

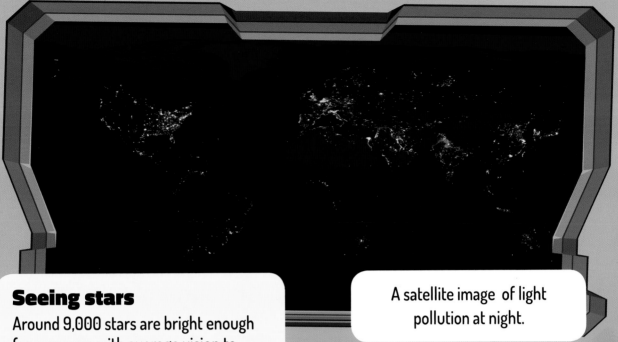

Seeing stars

Around 9,000 stars are bright enough for someone with average vision to see at night without a telescope or binoculars, but you can't see more than half the sky at any one time. This means that on a clear, dark night, you could see an absolute maximum of around 4,500 stars. In most places the number will be much lower, though, as nearby nighttime light—for example, from buildings and street lamps—drowns out the fainter stars.

Measuring brightness

The brightness of stars and planets is measured on a magnitude scale. The bigger the magnitude, the fainter the star is. On Earth, the faintest stars we can see with the naked eye are magnitude +6.5, but with a small pair of binoculars you can see stars at magnitude +9. There are far more faint stars than bright ones, so using binoculars like this reveals up to around 108,000 stars across your half of the sky.

Galaxy gazing

Because Earth is at the end of one of our galaxy's four "arms," we can actually see the Milky Way in the sky. Except that most of us can't anymore ... today, two-thirds of the world live in towns and cities that are too bright for people to see the Milky Way. Many countries now have International Dark Reserves, areas kept free from light pollution, to make sure we don't lose our views of space forever.

The Alqueva Dark Sky Reserve in Portugal.

FACT 5 Dung beetles can use the Milky Way to navigate.

NEUTRON STARS CAN SPIN 700 TIMES A SECOND

A neutron star is the tiny, dense core of a star that has collapsed in on itself. Just as an ice-skater spins faster when they pull in their arms, a star speeds up as it shrinks.

Packed in

Becoming a neutron star is one of the possible ways that a star's life can end. Neutron stars are incredibly dense, which means that they have a huge amount of matter crammed into a very small area. A neutron star packs around 1.4 times the mass of our sun into a ball around the width of a small city.

Woah! That's a lot of spin!

Most of an atom is empty space.

No space

You are mostly made of empty space, and so is everything around you. This is because everything is made of atoms and over 99.9% of an atom is empty space. If you could remove all empty space inside the human body, every person on Earth could be squished inside an area the size of a sugar cube. A neutron star has had all its empty space crushed out of it, so only matter remains.

Pulsars

There are different types of neutron stars, including strongly magnetic magnetars and extra-fast-spinning pulsars. From Earth, a pulsar looks like a star flashing on and off—it gives out two steady beams of light, but as it spins the beams go in and out of view. Jocelyn Bell Burnell first discovered pulsars in 1967, and the team of scientists studying them first thought they might be attempts by aliens to talk to us—they even named the first pulsar "Little Green Men 1"!

Star finales

A star only ends its life by exploding and turning into a neutron star if it is a certain size—too small and it becomes a white dwarf, too big and it collapses entirely into a black hole. Our sun will become a white dwarf—when it runs out of fuel to burn, it will lose its outer layers and its hot core will slowly cool over a billion years or so.

A pulsar

It doesn't look little or green to me!

YOU CAN SEE INTO THE PAST

When you look at stars, you are seeing into their past. Because of how long light from stars takes to reach us, they may not even exist anymore by the time we can see them.

Long-distance travel

Light travels incredibly quickly, almost 186,000 miles (300,000 km) in a single second. But many stars are so far away from Earth that it can still take a very, very long time for light to travel from where a star is to where we are.

Our photos of this spiral galaxy, M81, show it as it looked 12 million years ago.

I can't believe what I'm seeing!

FACT 8

If you moved at the speed of light, you could travel around Earth seven times in a single second.

Sunlight

The sun is by far the closest star to Earth, but light doesn't travel to us from the sun in an instant—the journey takes around eight minutes. You must NEVER look at the sun directly, because it can seriously damage your eyes and even leave you blind, but if you could you would be seeing the sun as it looked eight minutes ago rather than right now.

Seeing the past

Other stars and planets are a lot, lot farther away than the sun, so we are seeing much farther into their past. Scientists using powerful telescopes can see stars so far away that the light from them has taken billions of years to reach us. In this time, a star may have run out of fuel and ended its life—but we won't see this change for billions of years.

Dinosaurs on Earth

If there are aliens somewhere in the universe that are capable of seeing far into space, they will see Earth as it looked in the past—how far in the past depends on how far away they are from us. If they are far enough away that light from Earth takes 65 million years to reach them, they would see our planet as it looked in the time of the dinosaurs!

FACT 9

STARS ARE BORN IN GIANT GAS CLOUDS

A nebula is a huge cloud of dust and gases floating in space. Some of this dust and gas squashes together and heats up until lots of energy is created. A star is born and shines brightly.

Pulling together

So what makes a cloud of gas form itself into a star? Well, at first, gravity—the same force that pulls you down to Earth's surface. Gas particles are very weakly attracted to each other because of gravity, and as they come together the force of gravity then keeps pulling in more and more gas.

FACT 10

Horseshoe, Crab, Cat's Eye, Boomerang, Bubble, Ant, Tarantula, and Stingray are all real names of nebulae.

Under pressure

As the gas cloud grows, the gravity squeezes it together and it gets hotter and higher-pressured. Eventually the pressure forces the cloud to start collapsing in toward its middle and it becomes a protostar. A protostar looks like a star but it is still forming, so it keeps pulling in gas and getting hotter and denser. This stage can last between 100,000 and 10 million years, depending how big a star is being formed.

Star birth

When a protostar's core is hot and pressured enough, the materials there change and give out a huge amount of energy. A star is born! It has begun burning its limited supply of fuel—when the fuel runs out, the star will die, but it has billions of years before that happens.

Failed stars

If a protostar doesn't manage to reach a big enough mass as it is forming, its core can't get hot enough to jump-start the reaction that turns it into a star. Instead, it settles into its new state as a brown dwarf. Brown dwarfs are something between a giant gassy planet, such as Jupiter, and a small star. They create some light, like a star—but they have an atmosphere with clouds and even storms, like a planet.

FACT 11 THE SUN IS A PRETTY AVERAGE STAR

The sun is literally everything to us on Earth—we couldn't exist without it—but it's nothing special in the star world. There are stars a fraction of its size, and others more than a thousand times larger.

The biggest

The sun is huge in comparison to Earth, but not compared to other stars. The largest star that scientists are aware of today is UY Scuti, a red hypergiant that is more than 1,700 times the size of the sun. If we could drop UY Scuti into our solar system in the sun's place, it would swallow up everything as far as Saturn.

FACT 12 Most stars we can see with the naked eye are bigger than the sun.

Yeah, well, everyone knows the best things come in small packages.

But wait ...

UY Scuti may take up the most space, but it has a much smaller mass than other stars. Interestingly, stars' sizes and masses do not always match up as you'd imagine—especially when it comes to giant stars. The star R136a1 is only around 30 times the size of the sun but has 265 times its mass. UY Scuti is lightweight in comparison, with only 30 times the sun's mass.

The smallest

The smallest star ever discovered is EBLM J0555-57Ab, and scientists think it is as small as a star can be. If a star doesn't get to a high enough mass as it is forming, it will become a brown dwarf rather than a star. EBLM J0555-57Ab is only a touch bigger than Saturn, which would fit into the sun around 1,600 times over. It is a very faint star, around 2,000–3,000 times fainter than the sun.

Alpha Centauri has two main stars and a third, fainter one tagging along too.

FACT 13

The closest stars to our sun are over 4 light-years away. They are a set of three stars called Alpha Centauri.

Lone star

The sun does stand out from other stars in one way—it doesn't have any friends. Most stars have a companion star not too far away, and some are part of a system of three or four stars. Nearly all stars form with a companion, so scientists think the sun might have lost one at some point.

STARS HAVE STARQUAKES LIKE OUR EARTHQUAKES

Have you ever felt an earthquake? The ground shakes as the plates making up Earth's outer layer shift around. Something similar happens on certain stars, but it's more powerful than an earthquake.

Mysterious magnetars

Starquakes take place on magnetars—small, very dense, strongly magnetic stars. A magnetar is a mysterious type of star—scientists have only ever identified 23 of them. It has by far the strongest magnetic field of any object in the universe, and scientists think it is the core that remains after a supermassive star dies.

FACT 15

A starquake sent out the brightest flash scientists have ever seen from beyond our solar system.

Earthquakes can cause huge damage as they tear through Earth's crust.

Ain't nobody stronger than me!

Core and crust

Magnetars are so dense that scientists think at their center there may be a hot, soupy core in which materials have been crushed into incredibly small particles. Around this core there is probably a thick, incredibly hot iron crystal crust that makes up most of the star's volume. The material deep inside this crust is called "nuclear pasta," and scientists think it is the strongest material in the known universe.

Bursting out

Scientists think that a starquake happens when a magnetar's magnetic field moves with so much force it rips through its crust. Apparently, the strongest material in the universe is no match for the incredible power of a starquake! The movement of the magnetic field also pulls the star's core like an elastic band, which eventually snaps—a fireball of particles and radiation shoots out of the rip in the crust.

FACT 16 Scientists have only ever recorded three starquakes—in 1979, 1998, and 2004.

A starquake in action

High energy

A starquake gives out a giant blast of energy so violent that one can affect us on Earth when it happens on a star 50,000 light-years away. In 2004, a burst of energy from a starquake disrupted radio and submarine signals, took satellites offline, and actually moved Earth's magnetic field. Luckily, it only lasted for a tenth of a second!

FACT 17 A BLACK HOLE CAN TEAR APART A STAR

In 2018, for the first time ever, scientists were able to watch an enormous black hole grab a star with its powerful gravity and shred it apart.

Black holes

A black hole forms when a large star dies and collapses in on itself. It has a huge mass in a small space, and its gravity is incredibly strong. In fact, a black hole's pull of gravity is so great that it creates a one-way system into itself—it draws in objects and light, which can then never escape.

FACT 18 There is a black hole, named Sagittarius A, in the middle of our galaxy.

Yikes!

Mwahahahaha, you can't get away!

Finding proof

Scientists have believed for a while that black holes are capable of destroying stars caught at their edge. They worked out that this would create an enormous blast and send a jet of matter shooting out across space at great speed. In 2018, they actually saw the jet, confirming their theory.

Seeing the invisible

Because no light can get out of them, black holes are invisible to us. Scientists use powerful telescopes and special equipment to find them in space. They look at how stars and other matter in an area of space moves—when there is a black hole, they spin around it and create a flat disk. The spinning matter gives off different types of radiation that scientists can record.

Don't panic!

A black hole sounds terrifying—invisible, destructive, with enough power to tear apart a star. But it doesn't zoom around the universe looking for its next kill and although it has very strong pulling power, it can't suck in stars and planets from anywhere in space. A black hole can only destroy a star that passes very close to its edge.

FACT 19

Until 1967, black holes did not have one set name—scientists called them different things, including "collapsar" and "frozen star."

I'm panicking!

YOU ARE MADE OF STARDUST

Most of the basic materials that make up our bodies were formed in stars over billions of years and journeyed across the universe when stars exploded.

That's where we come from.

Human elements

An element is a material that cannot be broken down into any simpler substance. The human body is mostly made up of four elements, which are oxygen, carbon, hydrogen, and nitrogen. We also contain smaller amounts of many other elements, including calcium, sodium, chlorine, copper, tin, iron, and zinc.

The stuff of stars

Scientists can work out what a star is made of by looking at the light that it gives out. Every element within a star gives out light of a different wavelength, so by measuring the bright and dark patches of a star's light, scientists can work out which elements it contains. Scientists have found that humans and stars share almost all of the same elements, although not in the same amounts.

Zinc is one of the elements that makes up both our galaxy and our body.

Multiple lifetimes

When certain stars approach the end of their life, they push out most of their mass in a huge explosion called a supernova. This matter is then recycled to create new stars, which eventually go supernova too and continue this cycle.

The Big Bang

Scientists think it is also possible that some of the hydrogen in our bodies actually came from the Big Bang—the huge explosion that created the universe. In the early days of the universe, only the very lightest elements, hydrogen and helium, existed—they still make up 98% of the universe today. Over time, stars created other, heavier elements by squeezing atoms together in their hot, high-pressure cores.

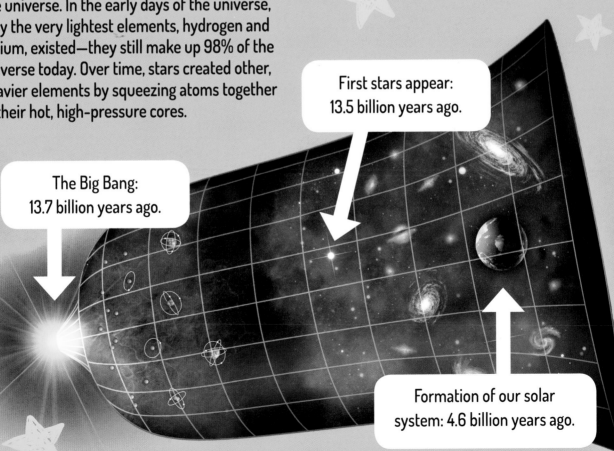

First stars appear: 13.5 billion years ago.

The Big Bang: 13.7 billion years ago.

Formation of our solar system: 4.6 billion years ago.

THE UNIVERSE ISN'T MAKING MANY NEW STARS

Scientists believe that half of all the stars that have ever existed were created between 9 and 11 billion years ago. The rate of new stars being born has fallen hugely since then.

Slacking off

An international team of scientists found in 2012 that since the universe's star-making peak 11 billion years ago, it has really been slacking off. The star birth rate has dropped by 97% from that peak to its current slump today. If this same trend continues, it will mean that 95% of all stars that will ever exist in the universe have been born already.

The Pillars of Creation is an area of space that has birthed many new stars, but it may be well past its peak now.

Hi-tech study

The team of scientists who made this discovery used three advanced telescopes to collect around ten times as much information as any previous similar study. They looked at a range of star-making galaxies at different distances from Earth, and were able to work out how quickly stars were forming at various points in the universe's history by measuring the light from clouds of gas and dust in these galaxies.

The Subaru telescope in Hawaii was used to discover the falling star birth rate.

Life cycle of a star

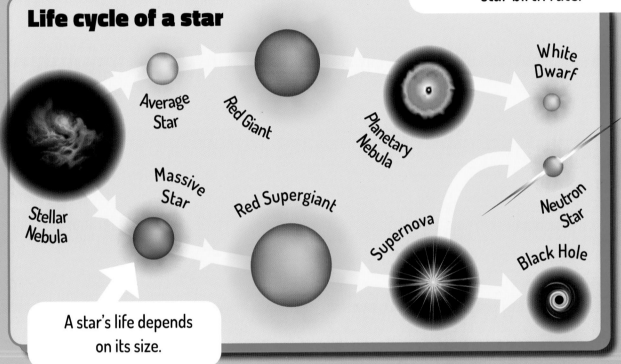

Average Star

Red Giant

Planetary Nebula

White Dwarf

Stellar Nebula

Massive Star

Red Supergiant

Supernova

Neutron Star

Black Hole

A star's life depends on its size.

Healthy galaxy

Many of the universe's billions of galaxies may no longer be forming stars, but our galaxy—the Milky Way—is in pretty good shape. Lucky us! As one of the universe's healthy, star-birthing galaxies, the Milky Way will play an important part in the universe's future.

Why so slow?

We are not sure why the star birth rate has slowed so much over time, but a 2017 study suggests that magnetic fields might be to blame. Scientists created a computer simulation of a particular galaxy—using all the known information about it to make their model as accurate as possible—and found that magnetic forces in the middle of the galaxy stopped its clouds of dust and gas from collapsing and forming stars.

EVEN MORE FACTS!

You've found out lots about stars, but there's always more to discover! Boost your knowledge here with even more facts.

Stars don't really twinkle. They only appear to twinkle in the sky because the different temperatures and densities of Earth's atmosphere deflect the light and make it zigzag on its way to our eyes.

The sun is classified as a yellow dwarf star. These types of stars convert hydrogen to helium in their core by nuclear fusion. The sun fuses about 600 million tons of hydrogen to helium every second.

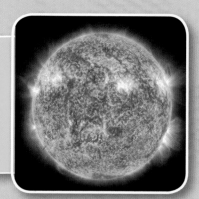

To travel to the nearest star system on Earth, the Alpha Centauri group, using the latest space probe technology, it would take about 75,000 years. The Alpha Centauri group is about 4.3 light-years away.

The most common stars are red dwarfs. They burn their fuel very slowly, so they live longer than other types of stars. They're also cooler than other types of stars, so they shine less, and they often have dark sunspots. Red dwarfs are less than half the size and mass of our sun.

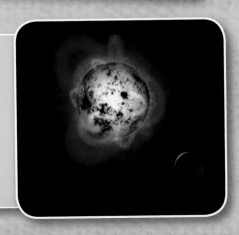

The biggest types of stars are red hypergiants. Two hypergiant stars have been discovered with huge discs around them. This illustration shows the size of our solar system compared to a hypergiant star surrounded by a disc.

Supergiant and hypergiant stars have shorter lives than smaller stars because they use up their fuel at a faster rate. They end their lives in a big explosion, called a supernova.

A star's color depends on its temperature. From highest to lowest temperature, stars can be blue, white, yellow, orange, red, or the coolest color, brown.

The ancient Greek astronomer Ptolemy (AD 100-170) wrote a book explaining the Greek view of the universe, in which the planets and sun moved around Earth. Ptolemy also listed 48 constellations, or patterns of stars when seen from the Earth.

The most visible constellation is Orion, which Ptolemy named after a hunter from Greek mythology, as the stars can look like a hunter with a shield and sword raised in the air.

Sailors used stars to navigate. The North Star, or Polaris, is the brightest star in the constellation Ursa Minor, or Little Bear. Since it appears above the North Pole, sailors could use it to work out their position.

THE STARS GLOSSARY

astronomer A scientist who studies the stars, planets, and other natural objects in space.

atmosphere A shell of gases kept around a planet, star, or other object by its gravity.

Big Bang The way in which many scientists believe the universe began—a huge, hot explosion that expanded out all the matter in the universe from one tiny point. Since this explosion, the universe has continued growing outward and is still doing so today.

black hole A superdense point in space, usually formed by a collapsed core of a giant star. A black hole's gravity is so powerful that even light cannot escape from it.

equator An imaginary line around the middle of Earth, at an equal distance from the North Pole and the South Pole.

galaxy A large system of stars, gas, and dust, with anything from millions to trillions of stars.

gravity A natural force created around objects with mass, which draws other objects toward them.

hydrogen A colorless gas that is the lightest and most common element in the universe.

light-year The distance light travels in a year—about 5.9 trillion miles (9.5 trillion km).

magnetar A small, very dense, strongly magnetic type of neutron star.

magnetic field The area around a magnet, or an object acting like a magnet, in which the magnetic power to attract is felt.

Milky Way Our home galaxy, a spiral with a bar across its core. Our solar system is about 28,000 light-years from the monster black hole at its heart.

moon Earth's closest companion in space, a ball of rock that orbits Earth every 27.3 days. Most other planets in the solar system have moons of their own.

nebula A cloud of gas or dust floating in space. Nebulae are the raw material used to make stars.

neutron star The core of a supermassive star, left behind by a supernova explosion and collapsed to the size of a city. Many neutron stars are also pulsars.

planet A world, orbiting a star, that has enough mass and gravity to pull itself into a ball-like shape, and clear space around it of other large objects.

protostar A pressurized cloud of gas that is on its way to becoming a true star, but can still fail and become a brown dwarf if it can't pull in enough gas as it forms.

radiation Very small particles of a radioactive substance.

red dwarf A small, faint star with a cool red surface and less than half the mass of the sun.

red giant A huge, brilliant (very bright) star near the end of its life, with a cool, red surface. Red giants are stars that have used up the fuel supply in their core and are going through big changes in order to keep shining for a little longer.

THE STARS GLOSSARY
continued

satellite Any object orbiting a planet. Moons are natural satellites made of rock and ice. Artificial satellites are machines in orbit around Earth.

solar system The eight planets (including Earth) and their moons, and other objects such as asteroids, that orbit around the sun.

spacecraft A vehicle that travels into space.

starquake A violent shaking and ripping of the crust of a type of star called a magnetar, similar in some ways to an earthquake on Earth.

supernova An enormous explosion marking the death of a star much more massive than the sun.

telescope A device that collects light or other radiations from space and uses them to create a bright, clear image. Telescopes can use either a lens or a mirror to collect light.

white dwarf The dense, burned-out core of a star like the sun, collapsed to the size of Earth but still intensely hot.

FURTHER INFORMATION

BOOKS

Aguilar, David. *Space Encyclopedia*. London, UK: National Geographic Kids, 2013.

Becklade, Sue. *Wild About Space*. Thaxted, UK: Miles Kelly, 2020.

Betts, Bruce. *Astronomy for Kids: How to Explore Outer Space with Binoculars, a Telescope, or Just Your Eyes!* Emeryville, CA: Rockridge Press, 2018.

DK. *The Astronomy Book: Big Ideas Simply Explained*. London, UK: DK, 2017.

DK. *Knowledge Encyclopedia Space!: The Universe as You've Never Seen It Before*. London, UK: DK, 2015.

Frith, Alex, Jerome Martin, and Alice James. *100 Things to Know About Space*. London, UK: Usborne Publishing, 2016.

National Geographic Kids. *Everything: Space*. London, UK: Collins, 2018.

WEBSITES

Ducksters Astronomy for Kids
http://www.ducksters.com/science/astronomy.php
Head to this website to find out all there is to know about astronomy; you can also try an astronomy crossword puzzle and word search!

NASA Science: Space Place
https://spaceplace.nasa.gov
Discover all sorts of facts about space, other planets, and the moon. You can even play the Mars Rover Game, sending commands to the Mars rover and collecting as much data as possible in eight expeditions!

Science Kids: Space for Kids
http://www.sciencekids.co.nz/space.html
Go beyond our planet and explore space through fun facts, games, videos, quizzes, and projects.

Publisher's note to educators and parents: Our editors have carefully reviewed these websites to ensure that they are suitable for students. Many websites change frequently, however, and we cannot guarantee that a site's future contents will continue to meet our high standards of quality and educational value. Be advised that students should be closely supervised whenever they access the Internet.

INDEX